Nostalgia Road Publications

GW00660418

Buses In Colour - Volume One

EASTERN COUNTIES

Malcolm Gee

The **Buses in Colour** Series™

is produced under licence by

Nostalgia Road Publications Ltd.
Units 5-8, Chancel Place, Shap Road Industrial Estate,
Kendal, Cumbria, LA9 6NZ
Tel.+44 (01539 738832 - Fax: +44 (0)1539 730075

designed and published by
Trans-Pennine Publishing Ltd.
PO Box 10, Appleby-in-Westmorland, Cumbria, CA16 6FA
Tel.+44 (0)17683 51053 - Fax.+44 (0)17683 53558
e-mail:admin@transpenninepublishing.co.uk

and printed by
Kent Valley Colour Printers Ltd.
Kendal, Cumbria +44 (0)1539 741344

© Text: Trans-Pennine Publishing Ltd. 2005
© Photographs: Author's collection or as credited

Front Cover: *Pictured during its last few months of operation was this Bristol LWL5G pictured at Felixstowe bus station in April 1968.*

Rear Cover Top: *New to the Eastern Counties fleet in 1945 when it was given the fleet number LK5 this Bristol K5G has just arrived at Felixstowe bus station from Woodbridge in the summer of 1967. It was withdrawn from service later that year.*

Rear Cover Bottom: *With traffic restrictions in place this Bristol FS5G has no problem negotiating Lowestoft's town centre in May 1980.*

Title Page: *This Bristol SC4LK LC564 (6564AH) was an Ipswich-allocated service bus, which is seen outside the Eastern Counties' Foundation Street Garage in April 1972.*

This Page: *A nice shot of Bristol FS5G at Felixstowe just prior to a cloudburst in October 1974. Although service 249 did traverse Grange Farm Avenue, it was normally usual for it to display 'Circular' on the blinds. I suspect that I may have been responsible for changing the destination in this case.*

Right: *Seen at Great Yarmouth in July 1979 is this ex-Western SMT VRT/SL6G, acquired by Eastern Counties in 1973 and withdrawn from service in 1980.*

FOREWORD

This new book by Malcolm Gee reflects an era loved by many transport enthusiasts, the time when our national transport culture changed. Up to the late-1950s, rail transport had been the backbone of long distance travel, as well as being of vital importance in rural areas.

Buses had of course, been making great in-roads into this virtual monopoly from the 1920s onwards, but it was with the great contraction of the rail network after nationalisation in 1948 that they really became a credible (and sometimes only) alternative. In many areas, they became the life-blood of rural communities.

One area where rail suffered a major contraction was East Anglia, as many of the routes there were so unprofitable as to defy belief. As pruning took place, and when diesel locomotives and railcars replaced steam engines, buses were introduced on replacement services.

The Eastern Counties operation proved to be a credible alternative, and Malcolm began his colour record of the company just as the Beeching 'Axe' fell on the railways. His story runs from 1964 to the de-regulation of bus services under the Thatcher government, and it forms an interesting record of the social change during that time.

Alan Earnshaw, Appleby December 2004

INTRODUCTION

Those readers who know me, probably do so as a keen rail enthusiast but my interest from a very early age was in buses. I was born in Colchester and moved to Felixstowe in Suffolk when I was eleven.

Railways were changing at this time, and by the time I had started work in Ipswich in late-1964, closures and dieselisation had already taken their toll on the rail system of the Eastern counties.

So, when I bought my first camera, the transport subjects I wanted to film were rapidly changing.

My new purchase (for little more than £1) was a Kodak Instamatic, but this was the best £1 that I ever spent. This gave me sterling service and was a great improvement on the camera that I had previously borrowed from my father, which had a tendency to let in the light.

Of course, my photography was largely limited to the area near my home, and the bus company serving Felixstowe at the time was Eastern Counties Omnibus Co. Ltd. The origins of the company, which came into being on 14th July 1931, are to be found in the Eastern Counties Road Car Company Ltd of Ipswich.

This was a Tilling subsidiary, which was registered as a limited company on 30th August 1919 and placed under the control of Tilling and British Automobile Traction Limited (B.A.T.) in May 1928.

To it was added the Ortona Motor Company Ltd of Cambridge, the Peterborough Electric Traction Company Ltd and the routes of the United Automobile Services Ltd that lay in Norfolk and Suffolk, as United in turn moved to the North of England.

By joining these four small undertakings in East Anglia, all of which were the subsidiaries of B.A.T. Tilling, it was hoped that the larger unit would be more efficient and lead to improved results. From the start the head office of the new operation was at Thorpe Road, Norwich.

Upon its formation in 1931, Eastern Counties Omnibus Company Limited owned a substantial fleet of 534 buses, although there was also a serious drawback due to the wide variety of chassis and bodies employed. Early withdrawal and replacement of this comparatively modern fleet was not economically feasible so the company adopted a programme under which single and double-deck buses were re-bodied and some single deck chassis were re-bodied as double-deck buses.

The firm then embarked on a policy of acquiring its small competing operators and by the mid-1960s some 70 of these had been purchased.

The most significant of these came in December 1933 with the tram and bus operator, Norwich Electric Traction. When the trams were abandoned two years later, the Norwich company was re-formed as a motor bus operation and re-named as the Norwich Omnibus Company Limited.

During World War II, Tilling and B.A.T. went into voluntary liquidation and in 1942 its property and assets were divided equally between two new companies, B.E.T. Omnibus Services Limited and Tilling Motor Services Limited. As part of the rationalisation that followed, and to meet the war needs Eastern Counties was allocated to the latter.

After the war, the Transport Act of 1947 established the British Transport Commission (B.T.C.) and the State was given powers to acquire transport undertakings, with a view to eventually integrating road and rail haulage and passenger traffic. As the B.T.C. already held considerable shareholdings in most of the Tilling companies, it made sense to purchase Tilling Motor Services from the Tilling group.

Like the other Tilling companies, Eastern Counties became a unit of the British Transport Commission in 1948. Outwardly however, the company showed no change from the Tilling era, although a degree of rationalisation was introduced in a number of areas. For instance, the company standardised on vehicles with Bristol chassis and Eastern Coach Works (ECW) bodies.

Eastern Coach Works Limited was situated at Lowestoft and was producing bodies for Eastern Counties and other operators. In 1936 it had been decided to separate the coachbuilding activities from the operating side of E.C.O.C. Accordingly, Eastern Counties Coach Works Limited came into being on 1st July 1936 although it remained a wholly owned subsidiary of E.C.O.C. The name change to Eastern Coach Works Limited took place the following year, and thereafter the company was associated with the bodies on many of BTC-owned bus fleets in England and Wales.

Above: *This Bristol SC4LK B35F (built in 1956, withdrawn 1970) is seen at Peterborough bus station in August 1968.*

Following major changes to the BTC in the mid-1960s, the Transport Act of 1968 resulted in the setting up of the National Bus Company (NBC) under whose control came all of the Transport Holding Company's subsidiaries, including Eastern Counties.

The formation of the NBC, on 1st January 1969, heralded the start of many changes in the bus industry and standardised liveries became the norm with the aim of presenting a corporate NBC image. This album covers the period up to deregulation in 1986. I hope the reader will enjoy the selection of photographs in the album and that they bring back nostalgic memories of the days when buses had their engines at the front and a running board and a conductor at the back.

Above: *When I began photographing Eastern Counties buses in colour during 1966, a plethora of 1950s models were still in regular daily service. Here we see LL733 (LNG 733) waiting at the Ipswich Old Cattle Market bus station in the summer of 1966, in the twilight of its working life.*

Left: *Fleet number LK277 (LNG 277) was a Bristol K5G, which dated from 1950. It is on the 201 service in Felixstowe during the summer of 1966, but it still carries the radiator blanket used to protect the vehicle from frost damage in the winter. A study of other pictures in this book will reveal the wide variety of designs being employed on the exposed radiator models, varying from quilted, press-stud blankets to simple roller blinds.*

Above: *The Eastern Coach Works became synonymous with the state-owned bus fleets, and was usually paired with Bristol chassis, but, this was not always a hard and fast rule! Here we have an ECW body on an Albion FT39L chassis NAH 973 from 1953. Seen here as fleet number N999 (previously N973) it is found at Ipswich Old Cattle Market bus station where it rests after working the 211 service. It is late summer 1966, approximately six months before the bus was withdrawn.*

Right: *Whereas the Albion was 14-years-old at withdrawal, fleet number LL713 (KNG 713), a more standard Bristol LL5G/ECW B39R was 17-years-old when it was withdrawn in 1967. Once again it is pictured at Ipswich Old Cattle Market bus station in August 1966, this time on the 232 route.*

Above: *Compared to LL713, LL710 (KNG 710) was a Bristol L5G 35-seater vehicle built in 1950. It is also pictured at Ipswich Old Cattle Market bus station in August 1966. The ECW-bodied bus was withdrawn in late-1966 and sold to the dealer Ben Jordan in March 1967.*

Above: *It was always frustrating for passengers and photographers to see a bus simply displaying 'Service', when the actual destination is elsewhere on the blind. Yet, this was a common occurrence when this shot of LC556 (3003 AH) was taken at Felixstowe in August 1967. Used for one man operation, drivers of these Bristol SC4LK buses had to turn round on their seats in order to take the fares of the passengers entering behind them. Alongside is LS786 (YNG 786) a Bristol MW for express services.*

Right: *This Bristol LWL6B/ECW B39R built in 1951 is pictured on the 96 service at Castle Meadow, Norwich in April 1968. This was a rather timely picture, as fleet number LL743 (LNG 743) was withdrawn a month later.*

Above: *Built in 1957 LC551 (VVF 551) was Bristol SC4LK/ ECW B35F used mainly on one-man-operated services. It is pictured at Ipswich Old Cattle Market bus station before its return run on service 224 to Bealings. In the days before 'white van men' gained notoriety, we see a Ford Transit parked in the background; it will be noted from its 'J plate', the picture dates from a very short time before the SC4LK was withdrawn in December 1971.*

Left: *This Bristol LWL5G ECW B39R was built in 1951 and became fleet number LL739 (LNG 739). It is seen here at Castle Meadow, Norwich in April 1968. This vehicle was withdrawn in December 1968, just prior to the incorporation of Eastern Counties in the new NBC.*

Above: *This SC4LK, built in 1957 LC544 (VVF 544) was one of two vehicles of this type that spent most of its working life allocated to the Felixstowe depot. Consequently it displayed both terminal points of the 238 service at the same time, as seen at Felixstowe Ferry in the late summer of 1967.*

Right: *On this occasion in early 1968 SC4LK LC514 (TVF 514) was working with a conductor on the crew-operated 96 service in Norwich. It was more usually operated (but not for much longer) by Bristol Ls. In the background more motoring memories are stirred by the 1966 Ford Transit van, and the 1965 Hillman Minx MkVI. Yellow 'waiting' lines have appeared in the roadway, but it is obviously still a time when people wore top coats and hats when they travelled by bus!*

This Page: *The bus chassis by Bedford were not to figure largely in the BTC-owned bus fleets in England. When dispensation was given to acquire small numbers for rural areas, the new Bedford VAM was acquired and given ECW B41F body work. Here SB664 (NAH 664F) and SB661 (NAH 661F) are seen at Norwich's Surrey Street bus station in May 1968. The Bedford VAMs joined the fleet in October 1967, but were withdrawn after only nine years service.*

Left: *This Bristol LL5G, fleet number LL735 (LNG 735) is pictured at Felixstowe in company with Bristol MW LM940. This bus had an eight-foot wide body on a seven-foot six-inch wide chassis. It was sold to the dealer Ben Jordan in June 1968 two months after this shot was taken.*

Above: *More successful than the Bedford VAMs, were the Bristol RESL6LX/ECW B46F buses, 14 of which were delivered new in 1967. Here RS652 (KVF 652E) is pictured at Felixstowe bus station in the summer of the following year.*

Left: *Further success came with the ECW-bodied Bristol RELL6G. New in June 1968 this example, RL675 (PPW 675F) is pictured at Felixstowe bus station in the summer of that year when it was working local services.*

Right: *This Bristol FS5G, LFS 31 (2931 PW) was built in 1962 and was photographed at Felixstowe bus station in August 1968 whilst awaiting departure for Woodbridge.*

Above: *This Bristol LS5G was acquired second-hand from Bristol Omnibus Co. Ltd in November 1968, and was one of a number of inter-company transfers between the BTC-owned operators just prior to and following the formation of the National Bus Company. On the Falkenham service, it is pictured at Felixstowe bus station in April 1969, but it will be noted that it does not have a route number blind.*

Left: *Due to its rural territory, dual entrance buses were a rarity in the Eastern Counties fleet. However, there were exceptions as we see from RLC714 (VPW 714H) which was pictured in Norwich in April 1970 whilst on service 96. All seven examples of these RELL6G 48-seater buses (RL712-718) were re-built to 52-seat front entrance buses in 1972.*

Above: *When new, fleet numbers LM640/1 (KAH 640/1) had ECW bodies perimeter seating and space for 30 standing passengers, however it is believed that they never operated in this condition. After storage they were altered to normal traverse seating for 30 passengers, but still remained high-capacity vehicles with room for an extra 30 'standees'. They had a short period of service in this form but before long they were once again put into store. Finally, after conversion to conventional 45-seaters, they re-entered service in September 1967, as we can see from LM641 at Norwich Bus Station in June 1970.*

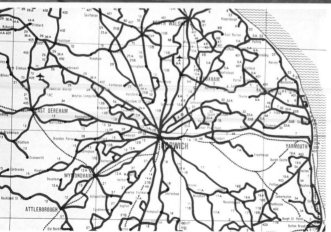

Above: *Ipswich's Old Cattle Market bus station was a favourite haunt, full of charm, character and an atmosphere that was full of the smells of diesel fumes and hot oil. Looking at pictures such as this, you can almost be transferred back in time as you hear the low note of an idling engine and see the vibrating tin work, as this Bristol LD6G waits with the 204 service to RAF Wattisham. Fleet number LKD212 (VVF 212) was pictured in June 1970 but it was withdrawn from the Eastern Counties fleet four years later and therefore was not re-painted in the new NBC livery..*

Left: *The extent of the Eastern Counties route network around Norwich is shown in this section of the company route map dating from 1972.*

19

Above: *Pictured at Felixstowe in the spring of 1971 whilst on the 201 service, this Bristol RELL6G was fitted with an ECW dual purpose body. This example, RLE869 (WPW 869H), in the buttermilk and maroon livery was delivered new in April 1970.*

Above: *Further variations of the buttermilk and maroon scheme start with CB845 (PPW 845F) from the company's coach fleet. This Bedford VAM70 was new to Eastern Counties in May 1968 and fitted with a Duple Viceroy body. The large expanse of glass on these bodies often 'baked' the rubber window seals, and water leaks inside the bodies were quite common. It is photographed here at Felixstowe bus station in June 1971, but it has a relatively short operational life for the company as it was withdrawn from service in 1975.*

Right: *Delivered new in March 1966 this Bristol RELH6G with ECW bodywork, RE891 (HAH 891D), carries another version of the buttermilk and maroon livery as it stands at Felixstowe bus station in May 1971.*

Above: *In the next selection of images, we present a series of views containing sunshine and shadow, with photography that is redolent of bus operations 30 years ago. Here we have another shot of the KSW5Gs that were once so prevalent in Norwich, as LKH320 (MAH 320) is pictured near Norwich Thorpe Station during the summer of 1971. It still carries its original livery (albeit quite battered around the front roof dome) and would not be painted into NBC colours as its withdrawal was fairly imminent.*

Above: *One of the 77 Bristol SC4LKs with ECW B35F bodies that were delivered to Eastern Counties between 1956 and 1961, LC565 (6565 AH) stands partially in the shadows at Norwich's Surrey Street bus station after arriving with the 33A service. Despite the fact that we are now in the Autumn of 1971, the new NBC liveries have yet to make a significant mark on any of the buses pictured here.*

Right: *Passengers wait to board Bristol LS5G, LS 777 (VVF 777) which is still carrying its buttermilk and maroon scheme at Ipswich Old Cattle Market bus station in September 1971. It will shortly work the 207 service to Colchester, whilst alongside we again catch a glimpse of RLE869 in a simpler version of the paint scheme.*

23

Above: *This bus RLE868 (WPW 868H) was in the same batch as RLE869 (pictured on page 20 of this book), but photographed here in the NBC dual-purpose livery whilst waiting at Norwich with the number 17 service to Lowestoft in 1972.*

Above: *Initially LE761-3 were dual-purpose Bristol LS5Gs, but they were demoted to service bus use in 1963, although they remained unaltered until 1968, when they were fitted with bus seats and repainted in the livery seen on LE761 (SNG 761).*

Above: *In all 105 Bristol MW5G 45-seater buses were bought between 1958 and 1966, but there were some differences in the ECW bodies. For example LM944, (3006 AH), which was built in 1959 contains a grille on the front panel.*

Left: *A 1963 Bristol MW5G, LM978 (478 BPW) waits in Norwich's Surrey Street bus station in the summer of 1972.*

Right: *In 1969 five Bristol LHS6Ps were purchased by Luton Corporation Transport, but were never used and were later sold to Eastern Counties after United Counties took over the Luton operation. As un-registered vehicles they gained East Anglian plates and fleet numbers LHS932-6. Here LHS 597 (WNG 103H) was photographed at Ipswich in 1973.*

Left: *New to the company in 1954, this Bristol LD5G was sold to the Eastern Counties Omnibus Society in Norwich for preservation in December 1971. Here LKD 229 (OVF 229) is pictured on Felixstowe promenade having participated in the Ipswich to Felixstowe run held annually in May. This picture was taken in 1974.*

Above: *Here we have an interesting contrast of Eastern Counties' liveries on a pair of Bristol MW5Gs at Felixstowe bus station in 1974. To the left is an unidentified service bus in the original company livery, whereas LS 784 (YNG 784) is pictured in the new NBC dual-purpose livery whilst supplementing the summer services.*

Above: *As the NBC influence grew, new types of vehicle began to enter the fleet. For their express coaches a move was made away from the traditional ECW designs to standard coach bodies from Plaxton and Duple. For instance RE853 (SAH 853M) was a Bristol RELH/Plaxton C49F.*

Left: *Pictured at Felixstowe in July 1966, this Bristol FS5G ECW Lodekka had been delivered new as fleet number LKD116 (FAH 116C) in September 1965.*

Right: *Definitely not a bendy-bus. This Bristol RELL6G, RL735 (AAH 735J), was re-painted into a 'brown paper' livery in September 1972 to advertise the company's parcels service. It is pictured on service 11B at Norwich in May 1975.*

Above: *Acquired from neighbouring Eastern National Omnibus Company Ltd in 1973, this Bristol FLF6G Lodekka (MVX 883C) was photographed at Norwich in May 1975. It carries the red and white NBC livery along with the standard fleet name lettering and the double arrow symbol.*

Left: *Another unusual second-hand purchase was fleet number FLF429 (LAH 448E) as the chassis and body shell of this vehicle had been used for test purposes by Bristol Commercial Vehicles from 1960 to late 1966. It was acquired by Eastern Counties in 1967, and the body was completed by Eastern Coach works in the February of that year when an LD-type front grille was fitted. It is pictured at the Old Cattle Market bus station at Ipswich in May 1975.*

Above: *Here we have a pair of former express service buses, both of which were originally fitted with dual-purpose seats. Although it still retains its roof quarter lights, LS819 (819 BNG) has been fitted with bus seats. It was also given bus-type indicators, converted for one-man-operation and painted in bus livery in April 1975, some five months before this photograph was taken at Ipswich. Alongside LS796 (4822 VF) still has coach-type seating and has been painted in the dual-purpose livery.*

Right: *Another photograph showing how former express vehicles were cascaded down to o-m-o bus operation in March 1976, as Bristol MW6G, LS809 (3809 PW) is seen at Felixstowe the following month.*

Above: *Taken on one of my rare excursions to Peterborough in 1977, this photograph shows ECW-bodied Bristol RELL6G, RL505 (BVF 668J) awaiting departure on service 333 to Gedney Hill.*

Right: *Eastern Counties also operated in and around Cambridge and it is there that we find FLF427 (LWC 665C). This Lodekka is another ex-Eastern National bus and it is seen collecting passengers in the city during April 1977.*

Above: *Fittingly painted for the Queen's 25th year in power, VR144 (GNG 710N) is pictured in the Silver Jubilee livery at Felixstowe Town Station (now Great Eastern Square) in the summer of 1977. It reverted back to normal livery in January 1978.*

Above: *Still less than six months old, LH 919 (TCL 139R), a Bristol LH6L displays a none too common destination on the Colchester 207 route as it awaits departure from Ipswich in September 1977.*

Above: *ECW-bodied Bristol MW6G, LS830 (APW 830B) has received the all-over white NBC livery and has found its way to Felixstowe on a day excursion from Norwich in June 1978. Sister vehicle LS829 is preserved at the Ipswich Transport Museum.*

Above: *Pictured at Martlesham Heath with former RAF buildings in the background, this Bristol MW5G LM621 (ENG 121C) picks up passengers whilst en-route to Ipswich with the 264 service in July 1978.*

Above: *Seen participating in the 1978 Trimley Carnival is this Bristol VRT/SL3/6LXB (XNG 205S) advertising the Eastern Counties' 'Anywhere Tickets', which seem reasonably priced at £1.30 per adult and 80 pence per child.*

Above: *As the registration plate LFS 281F suggests, this is one of the 12 Bristol VRT/LL6G 83-seater buses acquired from Scottish Omnibuses Limited in 1973. This example VR309 calls at Felixstowe bus station en route to the dock in August 1978.*

Above: *Repainted in the National Bus Company poppy-red and white dual-purpose livery in 1973, ECW-bodied Bristol RLE872 (XAH 872H) awaits departure from Lowestoft bus station. It will take the 671 route to Norwich, and its more comfortable seating arrangements will no doubt be welcomed by the passengers travelling aboard that hot September day in 1978.*

Left: *Seen leaving Norwich bus station in the summer of 1978 with the 629 service, is a Bristol FS5G, which carries the fleet number LFS68 (68 DNG). Behind it the garage has a number of vehicles resting inside, including a Plaxton-bodied member of the Grey Green fleet, which is just leaving on a journey to Great Yarmouth.*

Above: *If anyone thought that East Anglia was completely flat, this picture at Norwich's Surrey Street bus station proves otherwise. Having just arrived with the 871 service, we see RS654 (KVF 654E), a 1967 Bristol RESL6LX pictured in May 1979 with at least eight other buses in the background.*

Right: *Another Bristol VRT double decker to be acquired from Scotland was this model SL6G (NGM 164G), which came from Central SMT Company Limited of Motherwell in 1973. This bus came to be VR327 in the Eastern Counties fleet, and it is seen here on a Norwich city service to Eaton Park in March 1979. Note the style of destination blind, as this 'Alexander' type was not especially common in the east of England.*

Above: *Purchased from National Travel, London in 1979, this Leyland PSU5/4R with Plaxton bodywork became LL840 (VYM 517M). It is pictured at Felixstowe in April 1980.*

Left: *The terminus at Falkenham Everetts Corner, where LH906 (XPW 906H), a Bristol LH6P is about to leave with the 256 service for Ipswich in August 1979.*

Right: *One of six Bristol FL6Bs delivered new to Eastern Counties in 1963 LFL61 (561 BPW) had a seating capacity of 70. It was fitted with platform doors in 1972. It is pictured at Norwich in March 1980 and was withdrawn from service the following year. Sister vehicle LFL57 is preserved at the East Anglian Transport Museum at Carlton Colville.*

Above: *As the 1970s progressed, a start was made on vehicle standardisation within the NBC fleets and Eastern Counties received its first Leyland National bus in November 1972. This was probably the nearest the army has come to Kirton since World War II, as LN783 (DPW 783T) is seen displaying a striking advertisement for Army Recruitment as it passes Kirton Post Office Stores on the 254 route to Felixstowe in August 1980.*

Left: *With dual-purpose seating and the white coaching livery, Bristol RELH6L (GCL 348N) lurks in the winter shadows at Ipswich bus station whilst displaying the unusual destination of 247 - Felixstowe Railway Station. This view would date from the early weeks of 1981.*

Above: *The integral bus designs of the Leyland National, built in a brand new plant at Workington in Cumbria, had both their admirers and their critics, Here we see the two styles of National, at Ipswich in June 1981. On the left in an all-over red livery is a MkII version, LN613 (PEX 613W) bound for Norwich, whilst the vehicle on the right, (HVF 549L) is a MkI model in the red and white paint scheme.*

Right: *Eastern Counties used their Leyland Nationals on some quite long-distance fare stage services in the late-1970s and early-1980s as we can tell from this view. Here MkII model LN617 (PEX 617W) is ready to leave Norwich for Great Yarmouth on the 701 service in July 1981; again note the absence of white banding on the newer buses.*

Above: *As stated earlier, much of the Eastern Counties network was predominantly rural territory, with traffic barely sufficient to fill a single deck bus never mind a double-decker, but this picture of VR292 (VEX 292X) at Levington in March 1982 suggests a different story. This service (250) from Ipswich to the Suffolk village rarely carried more than a handful of passengers, but a 74 seater bus on the route was not uncommon.*

Left: *Eastern Counties no longer operate services to Felixstowe Ferry, nor do they retain any Bristol VRTs in fleet. However, in July 1982, VRTs were quite common at the ferry as it was included as part of a circular town route. Here VR256 (PCL 256W) is pictured at the terminus.*

Above: *The scene at Ipswich Old Cattle Market bus station has already changed when this picture was taken in May 1985, as the old bus garage has by now been demolished. In its dual purpose livery, LH930 (WEX 930S), a Bristol LH6L waits its turn on the 202 route.*

Right: *Another vehicle in the dual purpose livery, and fitted for one-man-operation, is RE846 (LWC 981J) a Plaxton-bodied Bristol RELH6G. This coach, seen outside the Shire Hall at Woodbridge in May 1985, was acquired second-hand from National Travel (South East) Limited in 1978, Previously it had been painted in the all-over white coaching livery and was often used on long distance express travel between London and the channel ports in Kent.*

Above: *Pausing to pick up passengers on the Suffolk Showground in May 1987 is VR270 (RAH 270W) an ECW-bodied Bristol VRT/SL6LXB. Nowadays showground visitors are picked up and set down outside the showground.*

Left: *Is this a case of all passengers sitting on the same side of the bus or an exaggerated camber of the road? This VRT/SL2/6LX sets down passengers at Felixstowe bus station in July 1987. There is a tentative link between this picture and the book's editor, as he once drove OCK 998K when it was in service with Ribble in Cumbria, however he tells me that although this was the first double-decker he ever drove, it was only a shunting movement of a couple of yards to free a tour coach he was taking round the Lake District.*

Above: *From the exposed radiators of the post-war buses that we saw at the start of this book, we have moved into a new era of both bus types and services. For instance, the 1980s and the rise in car-ownership saw the introduction of many new minibus services. An example of this type is seen with MA716 (C716 BEX) at Norwich Thorpe railway station in June 1987.*

Right: *Although passengers had shrunk on many rural and urban routes, these Ford Transit 190Ds were not really large enough for the job that they were expected to perform. This one, TH891 (C891 DEX) is seen at Felixstowe bus station in May 1988 on the 71 service to Grange Farm. Larger Mercedes Benz vehicles subsequently took over this service.*

Not really intended for narrow rural roads, VR242 (JAH 242V) is seen at Falkenham in March 1985 having travelled half a mile from the terminus at Everetts Corner.

ACKNOWLEDGMENTS

I wish to acknowledge the significant help I gained from the publication entitled *Eastern Counties Omnibus Company Limited – Fleet History 2PF1*, compiled jointly by the PSV Circle, The Omnibus Society and the Eastern Counties Omnibus Society, both in putting together the brief history of the formation of the company as contained in the foreword and also in references to the introduction and disposal dates of vehicles, photographs of which appear in this book.

I also acknowledge the assistance in compiling the history of the company I got from the publication *Ian Allan abc British Bus Fleets – 4 East Anglia*, which was published in February 1965.

Can I also say thank you to Robert Berry, Richard Haughey and Alan Earnshaw for checking through my text, and to Larraine Earnshaw and David Townend for the proof-reading. Their help has enabled me to bring to publication my personal memories of a great bus company, but most of all can I say thank you to you the reader for purchasing this book!